To -
Aunt
Chris
1972

From - Brad,
Vanessa,
and Brian
Dillion

D0991344

RIVERS OF
THOUGHT

TO
  MY
    ALICE . . .

RIVERS OF THOUGHT

MARTIN BUXBAUM
With illustrations by Richard Cuffari

This is a companion to the book
The Underside of Heaven

THE WORLD PUBLISHING COMPANY
New York and Cleveland

When I was young, so very young . . .
I used to dream and plan . . .
Of all the things that I would do . . .
When I became a man . . .

—from "Dreams"

Fifteenth Printing

Copyright © 1960 by Martin Buxbaum
Illustrations Copyright © 1970 by Richard Cuffari

Library of Congress
Catalog Card No. 59-11032

Printed in the U.S.A.

WORLD PUBLISHING
TIMES MIRROR

As the river of my thought flows on . . .
through valleys of my life . . .
so fast in utter happiness . . .
so angrily in strife.
So very, very slow in grief . . .
so musically in love . . .
so flow all rivers guided . . .
by the knowing God above.

—Martin Buxbaum

Emotion

*EMOTION is a pair of scales
upon which the soul rests*

*On one side are fears, pain,
frustration,
grief and despair*

*On the other, courage,
love, joy,
contentment,
and excitement*

*And however far the scales may dip
on either side
so will they in time
dip equally to the other*

*And when they dip we taste
the sweetness or bitterness
of life*

*But when they balance
there is no taste
but the blandness of monotony.*

. . . and this is the way
it was intended to be
we loving them
and God loving us
faults and all

the

inspirational...

Genesis

*F*ROM the earth, I scooped a hollow
. . . Filled it up with water, cool . . .
Birds, like angels, gathered 'round me
. . . Watched me build my garden pool.

*Life, by twos, I placed within it . . . in
my world of liquid space . . . Snails I
chose to do the labor . . . Fish to please
me with their grace.*

*Then I added swirling lilies . . . Mossy
rocks, both large and small . . . Saw the
beauty, slowly forming . . . Pleased was
I and loved it all.*

*With my task at last completed . . .
Down beside the pool I knelt . . . Looked
upon the life below me . . . Knew how
God, Himself, had felt.*

Worth

*WE can curse the fate that made us
. . . or love each living hour . . . if we
do the job God gave us . . . be we
humble weed or flower.*

*For each of us is needed . . . and each
of us has worth . . . or He never would
have bothered . . . to honor us with
birth.*

*There is fragrance in the roses . . .
and shade beneath the pine . . . and
softness in the clover . . . and food
upon the vine.*

*And each one serves a different need
. . . just as you and I . . . be we creeping
in the valley . . . or climbing to the sky.*

two *Glances*

*HER hands, her heart and every mite
. . . of energy she spent each day . . .
toiling with unselfish plan . . . then in
the twilight she would pray: . . . "Thank
Thee, Lord, for pleasant hours."*

*And He smiled on her . . . as He does
His flowers . . . and blessed her where
she lay.*

*Another lay and watched the sun . . .
come blazing up and fretting sighed:
. . . "Another dawn of tiresome day . . .
with nothing at all to do," she lied . . .
and tossing, cursed the dragging hours.*

*And He gazed at her . . . as He does His
flowers . . . and slowly turned away.*

Giving

*THE world has many happy folk . . .
who smile each day they live . . .
because they know that happiness . . .
depends on what you give.*

*For a giving man is different from his
neighbors in the pod . . . when his
thoughts are of his brothers . . . then
he's closest to his God.*

*And the spark of love he kindles . . .
in a breast where hope has died . . .
sheds a warmth that's like no other . . .
for it feels so good inside.*

*And every time he gives a bit . . . he
adds a little part . . . to that something
deep within him . . . that the poets
call—a heart.*

the Seasons

SPRING *is a time of dancing feet*
. . . and rivulets on city streets . . . of
laughing kisses, hair unfurled . . .
Spring is the time when boy meets girl!

SUMMER'S *the time of beach and*
pool . . . shady forests, dark and cool
. . . strawberries, topped with fluffy
cream . . . Summer's the time to sit and
dream.

FALL *is the time when canning's*
done . . . cooler the eye of the noonday
sun . . . bright is the leaf on every tree
. . . gone is the sound of the honey bee.

WINTER'S *the time for woody smoke*
. . . naked the branch of every oak . . .
white is the snow for miles around . . .
Winter's the time for quiet sound

Spring

DEEP whisperings inside
of a restless mind
would tell of Spring
e'en were I blind!

May

THE old and white-haired Locust . . .
spills its perfume on the air . . .
while the Dogwood lifts its crosses . . .
saying, "God is everywhere!"

the Harvest

ALL the garden's in the pantry . . .
. . . just the stubble's in the field . . .
Jars of jewels by busy housewife . . .
holding many winter meals.

Tomatoes—red as maiden's lips . . .
stare at sauerkraut . . . Baby limas,
crowded, waiting . . . Wrinkled peppers,
looking out.

Filmy dill spreads out to cover . . .
naked pickles, blushing green . . .
Carrots standing up like soldiers . . .
next to fraternizing bean.

Those who toiled respect this harvest
. . . they and nature helped to grow . . .
and remember hours of labor . . . spent
above demanding hoe.

Fertile land, like other blessings . . .
given to the great and small . . . if
unused, reverts to tangle . . . quite
impassable to all.

Those who seed their lives with
kindness . . . often gather harvests
great . . . and they feel a deep
compassion . . . for the ones who
planted late.

the Mountains
and the Valleys

NO life is like a level road . . . with
Heaven as its farthest goal . . . but
valleys deep, and mountains high . . .
that test your patience and your soul.

The valleys are your days of gray . . .
when plans all seem to go awry . . . but
valleys we must always have . . . or
else there'd be no mountains high.

So in your valleys, patience have . . .
be like the heart within your breast . . .
note how it very strongly beats . . .
then wisely stops a beat to rest.

Life

LIFE is a wonderful thing, and sweet
. . . if we let it swirl around our feet
. . . and know that we are a living part
. . . of all the world's pulsating heart.

To make life's meaning firm and clear
. . . there are rules to follow here . . .
simple rules, as most rules go . . . given
two thousand years ago:

Deny no man what he wants to believe
. . . respect his thoughts, and don't
deceive . . . take him by the hand and
lead . . . and help him in his hour of
need . . . for all are equal in fear and
pain . . . we all shall die—and rise
again . . . and no man is greater than
another . . . in the eyes of God—each
is our brother.

Tapestry

*IN thy tapestry of life, O' Lord . . .
my thanks for every stitch. . . . The
friends who form the pattern, Lord . . .
and make my life so rich.*

the *Autumn*
Covenant

HE planted a forest with
His breath
and watered it with His hands
white as clouds
and watched the trees grow side by side
across the lands
as brothers
sharing the bounty of the earth
roots overlapping, entwining
the one into the others.

And through the summers, long and hot
the furred and feathered things
saw the friendly forest grow
in living green and wood
knitting their shadows every day
shadows to cool the baking earth
He saw—and it was good!

When Autumn came, each living tree
declared its race
in browns and reds and golden yellows
each complimenting its fellows
and this was the Autumn Rainbow
of the maple, ash and oak
this was the flaming rainbow
of which God, Himself, once spoke
and said:

"The Rainbow of the Autumn
is my Covenant with men
that bare though be the forest soon
there will be Spring again!"

Hands

I HELD her hands in mine last night
. . . so very thin and worn . . . but they
held mine just as tightly . . . as the day
that I was born.

Those gentle and expressive hands . . .
etched by work and care . . . have
folded o'er my bedside . . . many times
in humble prayer.

They've washed for me—they've fed
me . . . they've helped me be a man . . .
There's something of our Lord, Himself
. . . in every mother's hand.

Exploration

HIGH in the vastness above us
are sights
unseen by the average man
though the stars have been there
since time began
there are only a handful who seek

All of God's wonders and all of
His truths
with infinite patience await
in the earth and the sky
and the boundless seas
for men who can see with their souls

Faces

1

FEAR has a thousand faces . . . Each
one is gaunt and pale . . . and each
one screams, "You cannot! . . . For
'tis certain you will fail!"

COURAGE has many faces . . .
though it needs but only one . . . and
this one says, "Keep trying! . . . For
you know it can be done!"

Compassion

IF everyone were perfect ... in his body, soul and mind ... then the folks who had compassion ... would be mighty hard to find ... For each living thing that suffers ... is a challenge to the rest ... It's God own way of measuring ... the kindness in your breast.

Hopes

FOR what are hopes
but slender ropes
fastened to our dreams?

my Chapel

*THERE'S music in my chapel . . .
where I go each Sunday morn . . . each
bird is loudly singing . . . just glad that
he was born . . .*

*No church was ever built by man . . .
with carpets half so deep . . . as the
green one in my chapel . . . over which
the clovers creep . . .*

*The ceiling is of many hues . . . each
changing with the day . . . there isn't
any special time . . . at which to go and
pray . . .*

*The decorations live and have . . . an
incense all their own . . . and best of
all, my chapel . . . is right outside my
home! . . .*

*Yes, my garden is my chapel . . . and
I'm sure you will agree . . . that in it
I'm as close to God . . . as I can ever be.*

Weeds

"PULL those weeds," a friend
advised me . . . "Else they'll multiply
to more." . . . But I left them, strongly
growing . . . where no flowers grew
before.

For they made me think of places . . .
useful only to the poor . . . who had
filled these spots with living . . .
where there was no life before.

Hate

*A WITCHES' cauldron bubbles . . .
in a body filled with hates . . . and
brews the vilest evil . . . while the
specter, Madness, waits.*

Parental Pride

I LOOKED at my children around me
and each one in turn I embraced
Each one was a gift from my Maker
God has such wonderful taste!

Misfortune

MISFORTUNE is the turning under
of life's stubble
so that a new and better crop
may be sown.

Pax
Infinitum

*ADVENTURE has a lusty call . . .
drawing as filings, men . . . Drawing
with a force so strong . . . it sometimes
crushes them!*

*And from the thrill of battles . . . are
tales for the old to tell . . . striking
sparks from eager eyes . . . of youth,
who dreams too well.*

*Man is not a plodding ox . . . bound to
a circle, plowed . . . until he finally cuts,
at last . . . the right depth for a shroud!*

*Peace is a woman's wish! . . .
Adventure's for her brother! . . . and
thus the two shall ever pull . . . the one
against the other . . . until at last,
man could become . . . a tender vine
that creeps . . . then the only sound
you'll hear will be . . .
as every woman weeps.*

Grandfolks

M^y grandfolks were old-fashioned in . . . the
quaintest sort of way . . . They never
cared for nothin' but . . . th' things of yesterday. Their wood stove in the kitchen was . . .
just twice as big as me . . . It had the best old
woody smell . . . when it was lit, and gee . . . the
rolls that Grandma used to make . . . would make
you roll your eyes . . . and no one in the county
wide . . . could beat her makin' pies!

  At night time when the sun went down
. . . she'd up and light the lamp . . . and in her
quilted rocker . . . she would rock 'n' wait for
Gramp.

Pretty soon you'd hear the footsteps . . . yep—'twas Gramp a' comin' home . . . You could see his pipe a' glowin' . . . as he puffed the stem of bone.

In the house he'd shuffle slowly . . . in his chair he'd ease down slow . . . while the oil lamp it would flicker . . . just to kinda say, "hello."

I remember how they'd fold their hands . . . on cloth of checkered red . . . They never failed to thank the Lord . . . for givin' daily bread.

After dinner they would sit until . . . th' fire was almost gone . . . The cat would curl more tightly . . . and Grandpa, he would yawn.

Then they'd climb th' creakin' staircase . . . to th' bed of quilted down . . . How I'd laugh when I'd see Grandma . . . in her cap and flannel gown!

I remember, too, the hurts acquired . . . in adolescent years . . . how Grandma's hand seemed softest . . . as it brushed away the tears.

I hope that our grandchildren, too . . . will learn to love the way . . . the wife and I will live and act . . . when we're grandfolks some day.

and now,
the whimsical...

Pets

Now some like cats—and some like dogs . . . and don't mind their scratchin' and lickin' . . . but the pet that I like, admire and adore . . . is the one known to all as a chicken.

What pet gives an egg for your breakfast each morn . . . won't take off your leg with a bite? . . . or howl at the moon or an amorous friend . . . but retires like a lady each night?

She'll eat anything a human will eat . . . her conduct is proper and right . . . I've seen her go 'round, just loaded with corn . . . But never have seen her tight!

When her last egg is laid and is scrambled . . . our chicken friend still isn't through . . . like no other pet she will give you . . . her carcass in savory stew.

the

Adventurers

WE close my eyes, my mind and I . . .
then far away we go . . . into a Moorish
castle . . . or the land of ice and snow.

We fly around in rocket ships . . . or
sail upon the sea . . . There's no one
has the fun we have . . . just my mind
and me!

Some times we ride on chargers wild
. . . in suits of armor bright . . . or stalk
a striped tiger . . . in a jungle black as
night.

We've been a million, billion miles . . .
from Siam 'round to Spain . . . When
tired we open up my eyes . . . and we're
back home again!

Sunbeams

THE sun stretched o'er the horizon's
hill . . . holding his lantern red . . .
while his sunbeams ran, across the land
. . . to wake each sleepy-head.

*A farmer waved as they passed him
by . . . and changed his land to gold . . .
the sunbeams warm, then kissed the
corn . . . and chased away the cold.*

*A sleeping bum in a building's nook
. . . smiled as they stroked his head . . .
and dreamed of things, like bouncy
springs . . . in a wonderful, beautiful
bed.*

*They dried a butterfly, young and bold
. . . loosed the bones of the very old . . .
stole a kiss from a hatless miss . . . and
guided a lamb back to its fold.*

*Then 'neath an oak they stopped to rest
. . . quite tired from work and play . . .
Its shadows old, and full of holes . . .
covered them where they lay.*

Geeple

*O*UR Geeple is a chicken rare . . . with feathers mottled brown . . . She isn't much to look at, but . . . she knows her way around.

She spends her days just pickin' and . . . she has a happy time . . . A bug, a bit of laying mash . . . a tiny speck of lime.

I'll walk into the chicken yard . . . the chicks all run and yell . . . like I was something sinister . . . right out of Chicken Hell!

But Geeple—she comes strolling up . . . as friendly as can be . . . and boosts up all my ego when . . . she hops upon my knee.

I have no single sorrow for the other chickens' lot . . . I think of them in pieces with . . . some carrots in a pot.

Our Geeple, though, I'm sure will live . . . until she's ninety-two . . . because she's smart enough to know . . . what friendliness can do.

Sooty

*JOANIE calls him, "Dearest Cat" . . .
and Cissy calls him, "Kitty" . . . Rosie
calls him, "Sooty Cat" . . . and all agree
he's pretty.*

*Berty calls him, "Pussy Cat" . . .
Martha calls him, "Cat!" . . . Katy calls
him simply, "Now" . . . Mama just says,
"Scat!"*

*Me? I call him "Eight Ball" . . .
sometimes, "Blasted Pest" . . . when he
trips me in affection . . . or annoys me
at rest.*

*Shameless creature—always hungry . . .
and fickle as can be . . . why anyone
would raise a cat . . . I simply cannot
see.*

*You say you'd like to have him? . . .
this furry, regal chap? . . . I really can't
disturb him—see? . . . he's sleeping on
my lap.*

the Widdle
and the
Wynette

Oh, the Widdle and the Wynette were a funny looking pair . . . for the Widdle had an overcoat—but hadn't any hair . . . while the Wynette had a hat on, and didn't seem to care . . . that though his head was covered—the rest of him was bare!

Just then they met a Wample who (and though it's strange to say) . . . was as bare as any Wample who was just born yesterday!

Then the Widdle shed a soupy tear—the Wynette heaved a sigh . . . Of course, you know that's silly, for neither one could cry.

They leaned on one another, said the Widdle, "Dearie me . . . such a naked little Wample, I've never chanced to see . . . We have so much, so much have we, it really is a shame . . . that here I have an overcoat that's longer than my name . . . and you—you have a lovely hat—it really isn't fair . . . that you and I we have so much—and there's a Wample—bare."

So the Widdle doffed his overcoat—the Wynette doffed his hat . . . and put them on the Wample (who could stand a little fat) . . . Then the Wample walked off down the road . . . between the Wolly poles . . . The Widdle and the Wynette? They're home in bed with colds!

the *Birth* *of the* *Minotaur*

In ancient Crete they sacrificed . . . the maidens, young and fair . . . and fed them to the Minotaur . . . a monster very rare.

Now history calls them "maidens" . . . but it means the Cretan "teens" . . . who sewed up all their togas . . . just to make them into jeans.

They wore their hair in horsey tails . . . and slouched in marble chairs . . . drank Pepsicoulos by the score . . . within the village square.

Called the bearded elders "hairy" . . . called the armored soldiers "tanks" . . . Had their favorite gladiators' names . . . tattooed upon their flanks!

They screamed at Elvis Populous . . . each time he twanged his lute . . . and fainted when Pat Booneutos . . . tootled on his flute.

They channeled every chariot . . . and souped up every horse . . . and tied up every heliograph . . . with silly, teenage morse.

Now the noble Cretan elders . . . were a

very patient lot . . . but they saw that Cretan dignity . . . had really gone to pot.

So they gathered in a council . . . Each elder wore a frown . . . All vowed they must do something . . . to slow the maidens down.

"Their mothers are our wives," said one . . . "so secret we must be . . . No one must ever know our plot . . . Does everyone agree?"

"I have a plan," another said . . . "to use within the hour. . . . We'll say the whole of Crete is doomed . . . by a hungry Minotaur!"

"A Minotaur?" said one surprised . . . "A Minotaur?" said two . . . "We've naught but two lone antelopes . . . within the Cretan zoo."

"It's just a gag," the planner said . . . "It matters not the name . . . We'll say it's half a man—half bull . . . and belches smoke and flame!

"Remember that old cave, my friends? . . . The cave without an end? . . . They'd never find their way back out . . . to bother us again!

"Each month we'll take a maiden who . . . is noisy, brash and bold . . . and say she must be sacrificed . . . then toss her in the hole!"

And so they did—and so it was . . . that Crete became subdued . . . and even Elvis Populous . . . failed to rouse a mood.

Yes, Crete was once a real-gone place . . . where maids could scream galore . . . but all the hep-chicks disappeared . . . until there were no more.

I wept when writing of this tale . . . that's sinister and dour . . . for I have teen-age maidens, but . . . alas—no Minotaur.

the Bookmark

WITH *word and word*
and phrase and phrase
the loom within the mind can weave
its wond'rous pictures
without end

And should the book
be laid aside
the bookmark shows the rendezvous
where words and mind
shall meet again

Complacency

the Christians

*WITHIN a tiny raindrop . . . that was
very, very small . . . a billion things
went 'round and 'round . . . and
marveled at it all.*

*And some addressed the milling
throngs . . . said, "Listen, O, my
brothers . . . there are many, many
raindrops . . . but there's no life in the
others!"*

*THERE they lie
in a ragged row
a cat, two mice
and a shabby crow.*

*Each was buried
with solemn rite
'neath the rambler rose
with its blossoms white.*

*And over each
a tiny cross
shows the world
a Christian loss.*

the Storm Giant

*THE one-armed leaves hang silently
. . . The breath of the Earth is still
. . . and the only sound on this
too-warm night . . . is an unseen
cricket's trill!*

*The first scared breeze begins to run
. . . and bumps the leaves around . . .
The footsteps of the Storm, himself . . .
rumble on the ground!*

*There he is! His arms outstretched!
. . . His inky cape held high! . . . He
strikes the hills with flinty fists . . .
and sparks jump from the sky!*

*Each time he waves his cape of wind
. . . the woodlands bow and sway . . .
while his sweat comes down in torrents
. . . and beats upon the clay!*

and the
Romantic

Love is a wanting the other
so much
that a thought is the same
to the heart as a touch

New Love

*THEY pity us, my own, and think . . .
that we are "settled," "bored" . . . for
they have just found love themselves
. . . and think it unexplored.*

*These many years that we've been wed
. . . these many children, too . . . these
evenings when we merely sit . . . if
they but only knew.*

*They'd never dream we watched the
moon . . . just two and a guitar . . . or
saw the firelight flicker . . . on the
water like a star . . . or that we've
known the holiness of love so new it
scared . . . or kindled fires of ecstasy . . .
that smouldered hot then flared.*

*No, we won't tell them anything . . .
for they must learn as we . . . that
passion is a noisy thing . . . but love
lives quietly.*

Marriage

the Tree

Henceforth
there shall be such a oneness
that when one weeps
the other will taste salt.

IF man were made perfect . . .
complete as could be . . . then God
would have never . . . created the "she."

For man is the trunk and the branch
and the root . . . while woman's the
blossom, the leaf and the fruit.

Revelation

"*CARESS me!*" *said her hair, and*
flowed . . . so warm and living, 'neath
my hand . . . its fragrance and its
texture such . . . it turns my sinews
into sand!

Her eyes said, "Look into me, love . . .
and I will open—widest wide . . . to
show what none has seen before . . . the
promise waiting—deep inside!"

Her lips said, "Kiss me, long, and find
. . . how nerves can quiver, and entwine
. . . two hearts together, evermore . . .
and make them one—as wine in wine!"

And all of her said, "Cling, and feel . . .
my pulsing breath upon thy face . . .
Cling—while the earth is torn away! . . .
And free, thy soul flies into space!"

Wives

I WONDER if she really knows . . . how I appreciate . . . her good-bye kiss each morning . . . beside our garden gate . . . A simple thing for folks to give . . . before they go apart . . . the one warm thread connecting . . . each separated heart.

Her kiss tells me she doesn't care . . . for jewels or luxury . . . her happiness stems from the fact . . . that she is proud of me . . . And if my day's a happy one . . . I'm anxious as can be . . . to hurry home and tell the one . . . whose praise is all to me . . . But if, perhaps, I falter, or stumble on the road . . . I know that she'll come forward . . . and quickly share the load.

With wisdom born of waiting . . . and with patience born of pain . . . she's the half of man that moulds him . . . through any loss or gain.

Perhaps God knew man needed Him . . . beside him in this life . . . and couldn't come Himself, so gave . . . the blessed ones a wife.

Husbands

"*What is a husband?*" *some have asked* . . . *now that you've written* "*Wives*" . . . *Explain this creature, masculine* . . . *for which the female strives. Well, a husband, translated* . . . *means home and love and kids* . . . *a fence along the road of life* . . . *to ease away the skids* . . . *He's the half of any woman's kiss* . . . *the echo of her sigh* . . . *the extra warmth that's needed when the winter's in the sky* . . . *His muscles match her softness* . . . *his nerve offsets her fright* . . . *he's a solid, hulking comfort* . . . *on a black and stormy night* . . . *Be he beggar or a bushman* . . . *a bum or reprobate* . . . *she can make him reach the very stars* . . . *repeating that he's great* . . . *Here's the final definition* . . . *that I write upon the sand* . . . *a husband is a thing a gal* . . . *can make of any man.*

*. . . each babe is Divine Reassurance that God
still has faith in man.*

New Baby

*IN her eyes is the wonder of life, O,
Lord . . . reflecting the good that is You
. . . Her hands are as fragile as roses
. . . Her skin like the morning dew.*

*Our thanks for the gift you have given,
O, Lord . . . a bit of Your heaven above
. . . the warmth and the deep
satisfaction . . . that comes with
a baby to love.*

Parting

WHEN I shall see your face no more
. . . only these, my grief will know . . .
God, my heart, and the Summer sun
. . . and the winds that murmur low.

For I will dream a thousand dreams . . .
and in each one I'll whisper. "Where
. . . is she whose lips have kissed my
heart . . . and left her mem'ries there?"

Grief

WORDS are very futile things . . . to give a grieving friend . . . They fall into an emptiness . . . that only time can mend.

Anniversary

Some years ago, my very own. . .I took your gentle hand . . . and on a trembling finger, I . . . slipped a wedding band.

And at the time I promised Him . . . the God who smiled above . . . that I would always cherish and . . . appreciate my love.

These roses that I send today . . . repeat my earnest prayer . . . that as long as God makes roses . . . then I will always care.

to Alice

I wish, my own, that such as I . . . might write
a verse before I die . . . A haunting verse,
with lilting rhyme . . . sufficient to the end of
time . . . that those in love might always know
. . . the words my heart had whispered low.

But such as this I cannot be . . . a poet of
eternity . . . yet in my heart I keep thy name
. . . burning like a holy flame . . . I keep it there
for God to see . . . how very much I think of thee.

your Birthday

THE years fall gently from thee, love
... as petals, when the blossom's done
... I gather each one tenderly ...
and save the petals, one by one.

I place each one within my heart ...
and very slowly, one by one ... the
petals form a rose again ... forever
sweet, forever young.

my Queen

I'm just a little guy at work . . . no different from the rest . . . doin' what I like to do . . . and know to do the best.

But comes that certain time of day . . . when we all head for home . . . I cease to be a little guy . . . I'm leavin' for my throne!

To my palace—underneath the trees . . . filled with those I love . . . and guarded both by day and night . . . by God, who smiles above.

Attendants, small, await me there . . . I've only to command . . . and the royal pipe and slippers . . . are placed in royal hand!

But best in all my kingdom is . . . my Queen awaiting there! . . . The sun and I, we both caress . . . each silken lock of hair.

Her lips meet mine and quiver, as . . . her soft hands brush away . . . the lines around my forehead . . . worn by problems of the day.

This is when I envy no man . . . and my life is most serene . . . The satisfying moment . . . when his Highness holds his Queen!

Beauty

M ost gals all try their level best . . . to look like Betty Grable . . . and sadly cry, 'cause though they try . . . they never are quite able.

A gal who's homely as a horse . . . or fat as a balloon . . . or skinny as a clothespin . . . well—she doesn't have to moon . . . If she'll just look around her . . . and try to visualize . . . what made the married gals all get . . . those most attractive guys.

It wasn't hair unnatural . . . foundation, smell or paint . . . or anything they sell the gals . . . to make 'em what they ain't . . . You'll find that they used kindness . . . sympathy and love . . . and made him think that he was sent . . . directly from above!

So be strong when strength is needed . . . yet soft enough to yield . . . be close if life should wound your love . . . and help him from the field.

Stay by him though he have despair . . . and help him meet each test . . . and should all turn against him . . . still hold him to your breast . . . Soon you will be a part of him . . . his very core of life . . . Yes—it takes an awful lot— inside . . . to make a gal a wife.

Infatuation

YOU speak of love as one . . . might toss a pebble bright . . . to see it sparkle in the sun . . .

You tell me of his looks . . . yet love, is never found in flesh and bones . . . or even books . . .

I've listened to you . . . and I've heard . . . Infatuation—that's the word . . . A mirror that reflects your pride . . . and everything you want to see . . . with nothing on the other side.

the Awakening

You are so young, my son
that all
your troubles are as pebbles small
and of these, but a few

Your love is young, my son
and you
and she see all the world
through but a single eye
as once thy mother did
and I

Ne'er again will kisses be
as burning as of those today
or flesh be deemed so rare
for passion is a fragrance that
the winds of time will steal away

For time grants each of us, my son
a span of happiness so sweet
It's like an angel's breath!
A span in which the curtains
of all of Heaven, so fair
open for just an instant
then close again, 'til death.

Contentment

THERE'S a lazy time of evenin' . . .
when the air is sort of still . . . and the
porch chair's so relaxin' . . . when
you've eaten of your fill.

You can smell the purple lilacs . . .
made so fragrant by the dew . . . and
you listen to the crickets . . . talkin'
cricket-talk to you.

Then the blue that's in your pipe smoke
. . . meets the last blue in the sky . . .
the stars drift down beside you . . .
and contentedly—you sigh.

And then among the other sounds
. . . is one that gives you pride . . . it's
the singin' of your loved one . . . to her
little brood inside.

Then the young ones come to kiss you
. . . just before they kneel to pray . . .
it's the final benediction . . . to the
closin' of the day.

Toujours Spring!

Leaves

*WHEN all the funny little things . . .
that light and warmth and water
brings . . . rise—as if pulled up by
strings . . . and those in love trade
golden rings . . . and hear the songs the
crocus sings . . . feeling, as I, that
everything . . . should at this time be
given wings!*

*Then to each wonderous day I cling
. . . and cares of winter from me fling
. . . Full pleasure from this time I wring
. . . Heaven must be—forever spring!*

*SUN-KISSED leaves of every color . . .
shading trees that gave them birth . . .
one by one, fall in the Autumn . . .
feeding hungry, waiting earth.*

*Feed the earth that feeds the forest
. . . which in Spring is green again . . .
Living proof of resurrection . . . that
to die is not in vain.*

Thanksgiving Song

EAT up, my hearties, and pass the meat! . . . Laugh—and let's be gay! . . . Have some more of the pumpkin pie . . . for it's Thanksgiving Day!

Pass the cider, and fill the glass! . . . Toast the men of yore! . . . They won for us a freedom, lads . . . we'll keep forevermore!

Eat up, my hearties, but don't forget . . . to thank our God, today! . . . Be ever mindful of His love . . . on this Thanksgiving Day!

and then wistful...

Dreams

*When I was young, so very young
. . . I used to dream and plan . . . of all
the things that I would do . . . when
I became a man.*

*I'd have a castle fabulous . . . a ship
with banners bold . . . a herd of
elephants all dressed . . . in red and
blue and gold!*

*But ships, alas, I later found . . .
made me feel unwell . . . and castles are
the coldest things . . . and
elephants—they smell!*

*I dreamed of, oh, so many things . . .
as only children can . . . but somehow
dreams are not the same . . . when you
become a man.*

Actor

I'M an actor, dear God, just an actor
. . . who's playing a difficult part . . .
being brave when my heart cries
against it . . . because I have bluffed
from the start.

I must laugh when my heartaches are
heavy . . . and my insides are twitching
with fear . . . for they think I'm the
man that I'm not, God . . . gay, unafraid
and sincere.

Give me strength to pretend to the end,
Lord . . . 'til the last curtain falls from
above . . . I don't mind if You know
that I'm acting . . . but never the
others I love.

Pity

*PITY is the heart's own well . . .
from whence the tears flow—all unseen
. . . And in their flowing, cleanse the
soul . . . and leave each fiber sweet
and clean.*

Questions

WHEN I grow old, as I someday must . . . and the past is like a book . . . will I open up each page with pride . . . or be afraid to look?

I'm sure I'll spot each weakness . . . when the sand is running low . . . and so today I ask myself . . . the things I'll someday know:

Have I lived each day with gladness? . . . And lent a helping hand? . . . Have I paused each day for guidance . . . and followed as He planned?

Have I labored to my full extent? . . . Helped the weak and poor? . . . Have I turned away a single soul . . . who knocked upon my door?

Have I always paid my honest debts? . . . and never stooped to greed? . . . Are all men friends of mine in spite . . . of color, race or creed?

The things I've done and do today . . . in memory's chest I'll keep . . . and when I'm old, my Maker . . . will I laugh or will I weep?

the Land
of Youth

'TWAS the next lane—I was certain
. . . and my heart was beating wild . . .
to see again the place where I . . .
played when just a child.

But a hard white scab of concrete hid
. . . the mellow country lane . . . and
the oak in which I used to perch . . . I
looked for all in vain.

The meadow with its twisted grass
so soft beneath my toes . . . was gone
and gear-teeth houses stood . . . in
regimented rows.

I dreamed so oft of visiting . . . the
scenes of happy youth . . . my mind had
kept them constant . . . 'til my
eyes revealed the truth.

and the religious...

Aloneness

*HAVE you ever traveled far away
. . . from all that's near and dear . . .
and felt an all-aloneness . . . though a
million folks were near?*

*There are some who must have others
. . . and cannot comprehend . . . this
being with one's self alone . . . without
a human friend.*

*This shows that they have little used . . .
. . . the solace found in prayer . . . the
talking to their Maker . . . and the
knowing He is there.*

*Yet God is all around them . . . as He
has always been . . . but the doorway to
the human heart . . . must open from
within.*

Prayers

*A BILLION prayers or so, each day
up to Heaven go . . . and tumble all
about the feet of God . . . They arrive
in every color, some are bright and
some are duller . . . and as they fall He
gives a gentle nod.*

*Prayers selfish or conniving, all burn
upon arriving . . . and fall as ashes on
the sender's head . . . while those with
whine or grumble, cause the heavens all
to rumble . . . and drop to earth as solid
bits of lead.*

*But the prayers sincere and deep, are
the ones God likes to keep . . . to show
to all the angels near and far . . . He
sets these prayers apart, and to keep
them near His heart . . . He makes each
one an everlasting star.*

Six Golden Coins

Within a hidden pocket of . . . a baby's tiny soul . . . God's hand reached in and gently placed . . . six coins made of gold.

"I give to each some gold," said He . . . "and he who does not spend . . . will find that only lead remains . . . upon his journey's end."

I passed the years in childhood . . . in laughter, love and fun . . . When I stepped across to manhood . . . I heard Him saying, "One."

In pale moonlight I held her close . . . her eyes were deepest blue . . . My heart beat out, "I love her, God!" . . . He smiled, and answered, "Two."

One night she whispered, "Yes," that she . . . would be a wife to me . . . My heart sang to the heavens . . . and His pleasant voice said "three."

Our first child brought me happiness . . . I'd never known before . . . and as I knelt to thank Him . . . I heard him whisper "Four."

Years passed and then my grandchild . . . made an old heart come alive . . . and warm His voice that murmured . . . "That was coin number Five."

When I spend the last He gave me . . . It's then I know I'll see . . . the Kingdom of the One who gave . . . those precious gifts to me.

the
23d **P**salm
in **M**eter

The Lord is my Shepherd, and I shall not want . . . for His blessings so warm and serene . . . He maketh my heart and my soul both to lie . . . in all of His pastures so green.

His pastures, to us, are the ways of His life . . . with love as the comforting light . . . which helps me and all my brothers to find . . . our way through the dark of the night.

Beside the still waters, He leadeth me on . . . restoring His peace to my soul . . . These waters so quiet, He giveth to all . . . who enter the gates of His fold.

By the paths of His righteousness, there will I walk . . . for the sake of His holiest Name . . . and living each day as He wants me to live . . . I'll never be lonely again.

Yea, though I may walk thru the valley so dark . . . in the shadowy world that is Death . . . no evil I fear, when He's near, and I hear . . . the sound of His whispering breath.

His rod and His staff, they are comforting, too . . . and these are His faith and His love . . . and when I am weary, on these I will lean . . . on Earth and in Heaven above.

I stand before those who are enemies, then . . . a table for me He prepares . . . anointing my head all the while with His grace . . . to show that He sees and He cares.

My cup is now filled, and runs over with all . . . the blessings He gives from His board . . . This goodness and mercy shall follow us all . . . who dwell in the House of the Lord.

—Amen

Proof

"*Is there* a God?" my small one asked . . . "Yes, there is!" said I . . . "Just take a look up at the moon . . . floating in the sky!

"In all the countless centuries . . . it varies not a mite . . . but turns with God's precision . . . on its everlasting flight!

"And no machine could man design . . . as accurate as this . . . this infinite machinery! . . . A God, my son? There is!"

about children...
the Seed

THE seed of love grows slowly, and
. . . unfolds unseen, inside . . . rebelling
at the fleshy earth . . . It pushes it
aside.

The heart within this tiny seed . . . is
very, very small . . . and only God
knows why it beats . . . or why it's there
at all.

The seed of love grows slowly . . . in
a garden dark as night . . . then
blossoms on its mother's breast . . . and
lives within her light.

New Father

JOSEPH—didst thou feel as I . . .
humbled, awed and somewhat shy . . .
When thou knelt beside thy child . . . and
asked of Him—the Christ so mild . . .
If He made thee worth the trust . . .
When He raised thee from the dust?

Didst thou hold Him—fast asleep . . .
and feel the goodness o'er thee creep?
. . . Tell me—didst thou fill with love . . .
for all things here and up above . . .
and in emotion kiss thy wife . . . who
glorified thee in this life?

Did she in slumber softly smile . . .
and did her hand search all the while
. . . and when it found thine—did it
hold . . . thy beating heart—thy very
soul?

Blessings

*THEY say their prayers, our wee
ones do . . . I'm sure the Lord's
impressed . . . at hearin' all our family
. . . and relations gettin' blessed.*

*"God bless Mom and Daddy," . . . begins
each boy and girl . . . "God bless Auntie
Mary . . . and God bless Cousin Pearl.*

*"God bless Grandma Lyons . . .
Grandma Harrell, Grandaddy, too . . .
Bless Hamilton and Toby . . . though
Hammy's now with You."*

*Now Hammy was a Hamster . . . and
Toby is a cat . . . and Cousin Pearl's
a funny doll . . . What will He think of
that?*

*Yet—when God gives out His blessings
. . . He may get a smile or two . . . to
find a doll, a hamster, and a cat
included, too!*

my *Neighbor*

I have a lot of children . . . and, perhaps I'll have some more . . . they clutter up the living room . . . and overflow the door.

At night when I come home from work . . . they greet me, in a crowd . . . the wife, the bird, the dog, the kids . . . with happy shouts and loud.

Then in the house for dinner . . . that so many hands have set . . . when the blessing's said, the murmur . . . rocks the gates of Heaven, yet . . . with all the noise and bustle . . . of kids and pets at play . . . I feel—well, sort of lucky . . . that it turned out just this way.

I used to have a neighbor . . . you could almost hear him frown . . . when a dog went near his rosebush . . . or his grass was trampled down.

His house was filled with silence . . . and mine with noisy feet . . . Our house is always littered . . . while his was always neat.

Perhaps God knew we wouldn't mind . . . the extra care and labor . . . and so He filled our house with kids . . . and clean forgot our neighbor.

A Child's
Prayer

*I*N leafy beds, the feathered things
. . . fold their heads beneath their wings
. . . and say a prayer, for God is there
. . . watching every tree.

By softest bed, I kneel to pray . . .
thankful for a happy day . . . I have
no fear, for God is here . . . watching
over me.

Unwanted

THE selfish who like children . . . but
say they can't afford . . . would put a price
on anything . . . created by the Lord
. . . for who can tell the worth of rain
. . . or snowflakes in the sky . . . the
smell of earth—the gentle wind . . . a
moonbeam—or a sigh? . . . All these
things and children . . . are gifts direct
from God . . . as beautiful as bluebells
. . . that nestle in the sod.

*The laughter in a baby's eyes . . . the
coolness of its skin . . . it's the image of
your soul and you . . . that sets a fire
within!*

*Divinely precious gifts of God . . . yet
cast by some like lead . . . to wander in
the infinite . . . neither born or dead . . .*

and then there is
Christmas...

the $First$
C*hristmas* T*ree*

Years ago, by a stable bare . . . there stood a little tree . . . and the back of an inn and the stable yard . . . was all that it could see.

Two travelers came by it one night . . . one rode a donkey, small . . . They entered the stable, and later, the tree . . . heard a baby call.

The skies were lit by a blazing star . . . 'mid angels, dressed in gold! . . . And silver halos hung o'er the heads . . . of all in the blessed fold!

But the drab little tree, by the stable stood . . . its branches drooping low . . . for in all the splendor upon this night . . . it didn't even show.

Gentle angels saw it weeping . . . tears from every shaking leaf . . . and felt that not a living thing . . . should on this night show grief.

They dipped stars in the rainbow's hues . . . and hung them on the tree . . . When it blazed in living colors . . . all gathered 'round to see!

The Babe within the manger raised . . . His tiny arms and smiled . . . And to this day, the Christmas tree . . . still delights a child.

the Bare Little Tree

'Twas a bare little tree, such a bare little tree . . . as we brought it in out of the cold . . . and leaned it up there in the corner . . . and took off the tag marked "sold."

We crowded around by the branches, we did . . . all prickly and fragrant and green . . . and felt them and smelled them and all shook our heads . . . 'twas the prettiest tree we'd seen!

That night as we lay in our beds, wide awake . . . we heard a soft rustle and tinkle . . . like the bells on a wee little sleigh, so we thought . . . and a sound like the paper you crinkle.

We listened and listened and then all was still . . . not a sound did we hear through the door . . . so we jumped out of bed, and we ran through the hall . . . and into the parlor we tore.

The sight that we saw made us shriek with surprise . . . for the tree wasn't bare now at all! . . . It sparkled and glittered in fairy-like jewels . . . like a princess dressed up for a ball!

I've thought many times, since I've gone and grown up . . . that the bare little tree was so nice . . . and so was the one that sparkled and shone . . . It was fun to enjoy it twice!

Christmas
Elegy

THE feeling of love at this season . . .
stems not from a day set apart . . . but
rather the unbounded goodness . . .
when everyone opens his heart.

For a week and a day we are brothers
. . . together we kneel and we pray . . .
one heart and one song paying homage
. . . to the Babe in the manger of hay.

Together we give of our presents . . .
together we share of our bread . . . each
looks upon all with compassion . . .
and words are the kindliest said.

And God, in His infinite wisdom . . .
smiles sadly on us below . . . because
He knows that tomorrow . . . the spirit
of love will go.

Each man will withdraw from his
brothers . . . while a chasm between
them creeps . . . and only the rain in
the summer . . . will show that the
Christ Child weeps.

Gifts

*WHAT did I get for Christmas? . . .
gifts of silver and gold? . . . No—the
things that I wanted the most I got . . .
to have in my heart to hold:*

*The jewels in the eyes of my children
. . . in the light of the Christmas morn
. . . The silvery tinkle of laughter . . .
from Katy, our newest born . . .*

*The fond embrace of my mother . . .
striking the soul like a chord . . . The
gold in the hair of my loved ones . . .
as they bowed their heads to the
Lord . . .*

*The friends, who with infinite kindness
. . . smooth out the cares in life . . . the
heavenly gift, from God, Himself . . .
the love of my gentle wife.*

*These are the Christmas gifts that
last . . . deep in the hearts of men . . .
should all that I own be destroyed . . .
I could build on these again.*

the Child without a Christmas

When all the world is silent . . . on this holiest of nights . . . In a million beds, the small ones dream . . . of Christmasy delights.

But some awaken sadly . . . and their tiny hearts are numb . . . when they realize through tear-filled eyes . . . that Santa didn't come.

A bit of cold or hunger . . . are things they understand . . . but a Christmas without toys—to hold in heart and hand . . . means that someone has forgotten . . . that someone didn't care . . . that Someone failed to listen . . . to a very special prayer.

It's, oh, so very hard to tell . . . a disappointed tot . . . just why she had to be the one . . . that Santa Claus forgot.

WE LIVE on the Underside of Heaven so let this be our guide: God will know us by our blossom when we reach the Other Side . . . 'til we meet again . . .

Martin Buxbaum